TRIBES of NATIVE AMERICA

Crow

edited by Marla Felkins Ryan
and Linda Schmittroth

BLACKBIRCH®
PRESS

THOMSON
———— ✦ ————
™
GALE

San Diego • Detroit • New York • San Francisco • Cleveland
New Haven, Conn. • Waterville, Maine • London • Munich

THOMSON
GALE

Photo credits: Cover Courtesy of Northwestern University Library; cover © National Archives;
cover © Photospin; cover © Perry Jasper Photography; cover © Picturequest; cover © Seattle
Post-Intelligencer Collection, Museum of History & Industry; cover, page 24 © Blackbirch Press
Archives; cover, page 9 © Library of Congress; cover, page 7 © PhotoDisc; pages 5, 10, 11, 13, 17,
18, 21, 22, 25, 27, 30, 31 © CORBIS; pages 3, 5, 6, 7, 15, 16, 20, 23, 26, 28, 29 © nativestock.com

LIBRARY OF CONGRESS CATALOGING-IN-PUBLICATION DATA

Crow / Marla Felkins Ryan, book editor; Linda Schmittroth, book editor.
   v. cm. — (Tribes of Native America)
Includes bibliographical references and index.
Contents: Name — Origins and group affiliations — Peaceful relations with whites —
Language — Economy — Daily life — Customs — Current tribal issues.
   ISBN 1-56711-623-X (hardback : alk. paper)
   1. Crow Indians—Juvenile literature. [1. Crow Indians. 2. Indians of North America—
Montana.] I. Ryan, Marla Felkins. II. Schmittroth, Linda. III. Series.
   E99.C92 C748 2003
   978.6004'9752—dc21   2002008669

Printed in United States
10 9 8 7 6 5 4 3 2 1

Table of Contents

CROW

Name

The name Crow comes from a translation of the tribe's name for itself, *Absaroka* or *Apsaalooke*. It means "children of the long-beaked bird."

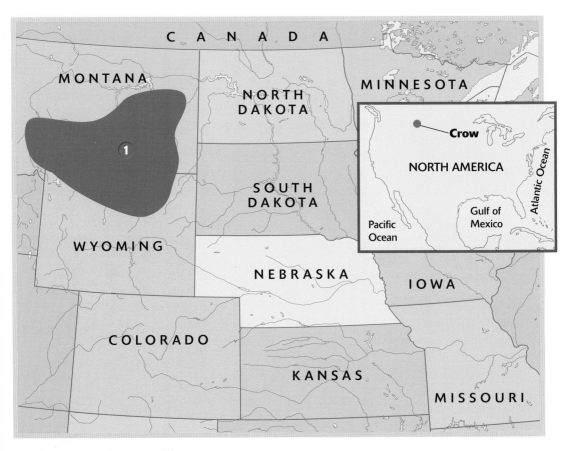

Contemporary Communities
1. Crow Indian Reservation, Montana
Shaded area: Traditional Crow homelands in present-day Montana and Wyoming

Where are the traditional Crow lands?

The Crow once lived along the Yellowstone River and its branches in Montana. Today, many live on the Crow Indian Reservation in Bighorn County in south-central Montana. Others live in the nearby towns of Billings and Hardin.

This 19th century painting depicts Crow people.

What has happened to the population?

Before 1740, there were about 8,000 Crow. In 1944, there were about 2,500. In a 1990 population count by the U.S. Bureau of the Census, 9,394 people said they were Crow.

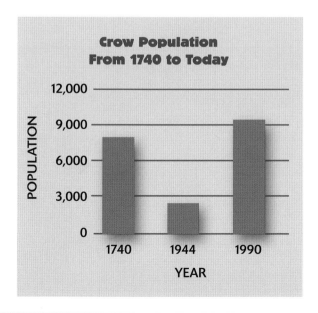

Crow Population From 1740 to Today

POPULATION

12,000

9,000

6,000

3,000

0

1740   1944   1990

YEAR

A young Crow boy dressed in traditional dance clothing

Origins and group ties

Crow tales say the tribe came from a land of many lakes—probably Manitoba, in Canada. Historians believe that before 1300, the Crow lived near the headwaters of the Mississippi River and as far north as Lake Winnipeg. At that time, they were part of the Hidatsa tribe. The Crow split with the Hidatsa and went westward. They entered Montana in the 1600s.

Before 1300, the Crow lived in Canada along the Mississippi River (pictured).

The Crow were hunters. The men were known as fierce warriors, but the people were kind to strangers. Although they cooperated with whites, they were forced to give up all but a small part of their lands. In modern times, the Crow people have kept many of their traditions.

Present day Manitoba, Canada (pictured) was the original home of the Crow.

Crow men were hunters.

HISTORY

Farmers to hunters

Early in their history, the Crow were part of the Hidatsa tribe. They lived as farmers. In the early 1600s, a powerful tribal leader called No Vitals had a vision. It told him to take his people west into the Rocky Mountains to search for a sacred tobacco plant. He believed the seeds of the plant would give his people a special identity and make them strong.

The Crow turned from farming to hunting buffalo after they left the Hidatsa.

The Crow acquired horses in the mid-1700s, which enabled them to hunt more efficiently.

In the mid-1600s or early 1700s, about 500 people left the Hidatsa to fulfill No Vitals's vision. They went to an area near the Yellowstone River in present-day southern Montana and northern Wyoming. They soon abandoned their old lifestyle to be like other Great Plains people. They lived in hide-covered tepees, followed the buffalo, and hunted for game. The new tribe became known as the Crow.

In the mid-1700s, the tribe acquired horses. Horses helped them travel, hunt, and fight wars. By the early 1800s, they had more horses than any other tribe east of the Rocky Mountains.

1876
Crow warriors act as scouts for Lieutenant Colonel George Custer before his defeat in the Battle of the Little Bighorn

1917–1918
WWI fought in Europe

1929
Stock market crash begins the Great Depression

1934
The Indian Reorganization Act gives tribes self-government

1934
The Crow refuse to accept the terms of the Indian Reorganization Act

1941
Bombing at Pearl Harbor forces United States into WWII

1945
WWII ends

1948
The Crow write their own constitution and start a tribal government

1950s
Reservations no longer controlled by federal government

Split into two groups

American explorers Meriwether Lewis and William Clark met the Crow in 1806. The Crow and other Indians and whites had come to trade near Bismarck, North Dakota. Soon, even more fur traders began to come to Crow lands. There, they built forts and trading posts.

In 1825, two powerful chiefs had a disagreement. As a result, the Crow split into two groups. Chief Long Hair led the Mountain Crow into the high

The Lewis and Clark Expedition met the Crow in 1806.

country south of the Yellowstone River. Chief Arapooish and the River Crow stayed north of the Yellowstone, along the Musselshell and Judith Rivers. As white settlers moved westward, the Crow had fights with other tribes who moved onto their lands. The Crow were usually outnumbered. Therefore, they rarely started wars. They did steal horses from their neighbors, however.

A Crow warrior rides through camp during a war with the Sioux.

Peace with whites

By the 1850s, more white settlers streamed into Crow country. At times, the Crow raided the newcomers. Most often, though, their relations with whites were peaceful.

Wars and smallpox epidemics killed many Crow. Experts believed the tribe would soon die out. Instead, the Crow settled on a reservation in Montana and began to cooperate with the U.S. Army. The Crow signed the Fort Laramie Treaty of 1851. It gave them 38.5 million acres in southern Montana,

Native American tribes defeated George Armstrong Custer (center) and his men at the Battle of Little Bighorn. Crow men served as scouts for Custer before the battle.

northern Wyoming, and western South Dakota. The Second Fort Laramie Treaty was signed in 1868. It set up the Crow reservation south of the Yellowstone River.

In the late 1800s, Crow leader Plenty Coups (pronounced *Coo*) had a vision. In it, he learned that his people had to help the whites if they hoped to survive. As a result, his Crow warriors helped U.S. troops in several battles. Crow fought alongside American soldiers against the Nez Perce and Sioux tribes in the 1870s. They also served as scouts for Lieutenant Colonel George Armstrong Custer

(1836-1876) before his defeat in 1876 at the Battle of the Little Bighorn. Crow cooperation did not make whites treat them better than other tribes. The army did protect the Crow from the Sioux, however.

A way of life shattered

During the 1880s, many miners, trappers, and settlers moved to Crow lands. They built forts and railroads. Whites killed buffalo on a large scale, and by 1883, the herds had all but disappeared. The Crow's way of life also came to an end.

This Crow man served as a scout for George Armstrong Custer in the 1870s.

The Crow were left without their main source of food and clothing. They had to depend on government agents to survive. Over the next few decades, the Crow reservation was made smaller several times. It was down to 2.3 million acres by 1905. At the same time, the Crow culture faded away. Christian schools on the reservation, and federal laws, did not allow native ceremonies to be held.

The Allotment Act of 1887 split reservations into individual plots. The rest of the land was opened up to white settlement. The idea was to force the Indians to be more like whites, who had their own farms. Many Crow did not want to farm. They had to

Whites killed buffalo for sport. By 1883, buffalo herds were nearly extinct.

sell their land to whites. In time, Crow lands became a checkerboard of native and non-native plots.

Crow culture comes back

In the late 1800s, Plenty Coups spent time in Washington, D.C. There, he met important people and became skillful in the workings of the government. If an official would not listen to his demands, Plenty Coups paid a visit to the official's rivals. They were happy to pay attention. He also learned that Christian church leaders would often come to the Indians' defense.

In 1911, the Crow formed a business committee to speak officially for the tribe. It was led by Robert Yellowtail, a young Crow man who had been educated in white-run schools. During the 1920s, a general council took the place of the committee. Over time, the Crow who went to council meetings became active participants in the process.

Plenty Coups worked with government leaders and Christian organizations to get aid for his people.

In 1934, the Crow took steps to revive their culture. The tribe refused to accept the terms of the Indian Reorganization Act. The act would have allowed the Crow to write a constitution, but only with the help of the federal government. The Crow chose to stay independent. In 1948, Robert Yellowtail led the Crow as they wrote their own constitution. They then began to practice their religion freely and to follow their traditions without fear of criticism.

Powwows—traditional gatherings that feature song and dance—are held annually on the Crow reservation.

Modern times

Today, the Crow reservation is home not only to the Crow people, but also to several thousand non-Indians. These non-natives have leased or bought land from the tribe. Many native people work for the tribal government. Money from the federal government has helped start health, education, and housing programs.

Religion

The Crow religion was based on the relationship between each tribal member and his or her guardian spirit. This spirit was the source of a person's power, wealth, and success. Guardian spirits took the form of animals or features of the environment. They usually showed themselves to a person during a vision quest.

Tobacco was a sacred crop to the Crow. It was sometimes kept inside a medicine bundle like this one.

The Crow believed that tobacco had supernatural power. It played a big role in their survival. Tobacco was the only crop the tribe grew.

Crow Indian Sweat Teepee.

Sweat lodges (pictured above) were used by the Crow for purification.

The people who cared for the tobacco plants were members of the Tobacco Society. They were able to influence events in the natural world. Only men were allowed to smoke tobacco. There were strict rules about the practice.

Even today, tobacco plays a role in Crow religion. The people also still use sweat lodges (buildings in which water is poured over hot rocks to produce steam) for purification. Although some Crow are part of Christian churches, others practice the Peyote (pay-OH-tee) religion. Peyote, which comes from a cactus plant, can cause visions and is used in certain religious ceremonies.

Government

Each band of Crow was led by one or more chiefs. To earn his position, a chief had to accomplish four feats. First, he had to lead a successful raid against an enemy tribe. Second, he had to capture an enemy's horses. Third, he had to take a weapon from a live enemy. Lastly, he had to be the first member of a war party to touch an enemy with a special stick called a coup stick. This practice was called "counting coup."

Most bands had more than one chief. A chief might have great leadership abilities or influence over the spirits. The chief might also be a good public speaker or be generous. When the band had a period of bad luck, it simply chose a new chief.

Today, the Crow are led by a general council. This group is made up of all adult members of the tribe. Any person of voting age can speak at council meetings. A tribal court settles disagreements.

Economy

The traditional Crow economy was based mostly on hunting. This required the Crow to move often. Before the Crow had horses, the people used tame dogs to carry or pull their belongings as they traveled. Horses gave them more freedom of movement. Their hunts became more successful. Before the whites came, Crow lands were full of

A Crow woman prepares an animal hide.

large game animals. There were huge herds of buffalo, deer, elk, bighorn sheep, and grizzly bears. Hunting supplied most of the tribe's food, clothing, and shelter. Women prepared the animal carcasses. They also gathered plant foods, collected firewood and water, and cooked meals. They prepared hides and made clothing and tepee covers. They set up and took down tepees when the tribe moved. They also cared for the children and horses.

Today, the tribe gets most of its income from leasing its land to coal, gas, and oil companies. It also gets money from federal government grants. Other income comes from timber, fisheries, and hunting. Although some tribal members have tried to farm or ranch, they often do not have money to buy cattle, tools, and seeds. The U.S. government is the largest employer of Crow on the reservation. Other Crow work as teachers, social workers, police officers, and cowboys. Some work in restaurant and coal-mining businesses. It is still a challenge for people on a reservation to find jobs.

DAILY LIFE

Families

The major social unit of the Crow was the extended family, or clan. A clan is a group of families with a common ancestor. In Crow society, descent was traced through the mother's clan. Clans protected, defended, and helped their members in times of trouble. To be told, "You are without relatives" was the worst possible insult to a Crow.

The Crow adopted the hide-covered tepees used by other Great Plains tribes.

The Crow had a strict code of behavior. A boy was expected to pay special respect to elder male relatives and to his father's kin. Other relatives were to be avoided. For example, married men and women were not supposed to talk to their fathers-in-law or mothers-in-law. Members of the same clan could not marry one another.

Buildings

After they left the Hidatsa, the Crow adopted the hide-covered tepees used by most Great Plains tribes. Each tepee had a cone-shaped wooden frame made up of 20 poles, each about

25 feet long. The structure was covered with buffalo skins. Tepees usually had a fireplace in the center and a hole at the top to allow smoke to escape. Crow families slept on hide mattresses laid along the sides of the tepee. They built small, dome-shaped sweat lodges.

Clothing

The Crow were known for their striking appearance. Crow men, in particular, were very careful about how they dressed. Their everyday clothing included a shirt, hair-trimmed leggings held up by a belt, moccasins, and a buffalo robe. For special occasions, they wore fancy costumes decorated with dyed porcupine quills or beads. The bridles, saddles, and blankets used on their horses were also fancy. Crow men usually wore their hair long. They sometimes glued human hair or horsehair to the ends to make it even longer.

Crow men took great pride in their appearance. Their leggings were often decorated with leather fringe and beads.

They often hung ornaments in their hair. They also wore earrings and necklaces made of bone, bear claws, or abalone shells. They painted red designs on their faces and put yellow paint on their eyelids.

Crow women, who spent long hours doing difficult tasks, tended to be less neat and less elaborately dressed than men were. Women usually wore calf-length dresses made of deer or mountain sheep skins. These were decorated with rows of elk teeth in front and back. Women also wore leggings and moccasins. They often had short hair. They either pulled it out or cut it short when they mourned the death of a relative.

Food

As they hunted, the Crow also looked for plant foods. In spring, they gathered wild turnips, rhubarb, and strawberries. In the summer, they looked for chokecherries, plums, and other fruits. Throughout the year, the Crow diet depended on rabbit, deer, elk, grizzly bears, bighorn sheep, and other game.

The Crow gathered fruits and vegetables each spring and summer.

In 1884, Crow children started to attend schools near their reservations.

Education

The early Crow had no formal schools. Children learned as they imitated adults. To help their sons become hunters and warriors, fathers taught them survival skills, such as trapping. Mothers taught their daughters how to cook food, make clothing, and take care of a home.

Beginning in 1884, Crow children had to attend a day school near the reservation. Some students were sent away to boarding school. Most children in these schools had to dress like whites and speak English. Conditions at the boarding schools were harsh, and some schools were so unclean that children fell ill. Despite pressures for children to be more like whites, the Crow made great efforts to hold onto their beliefs.

Today, the Crow reservation has three high schools. They are financed by income from coal mining. Two of these schools are among the wealthiest in Montana. The town of Crow Agency is the home of Little Bighorn Community College. Ninety percent of the students at this two-year college are Crow. The school associate arts degrees in fields that will help the growing economy of the Crow Indian Reservation community.

Healing practices

The Crow had two types of healers. One treated minor illnesses and injuries. He or she might rub plant products on sores or lance a swollen area. The other type of healers, shamans (pronounced SHAH-munz or SHAY-munz), treated major problems such as snakebites or diseases. To do this, they consulted the spirits.

Every Crow person had his or her own medicine bundle. This small pouch held sacred objects that symbolized the power of the person's guardian spirit. The medicine bundle was thought to be the source of health, luck, and power. Today, health care on the reservation is provided at a hospital in the town of Crow Agency.

A medicine bundle held objects that were unique to its creator.

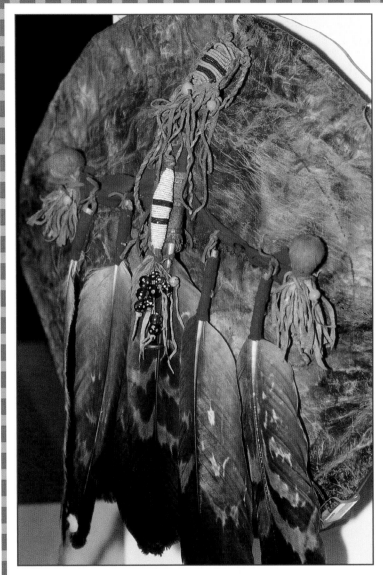

Crow carefully decorated their shields with feathers, beads, and buckskin.

Shields

The Crow carefully decorated the rawhide shields they took into battle. The images on them often came from an artist's visions. They showed his link with the supernatural. Shields sometimes had sacred objects such as feathers attached to them. They were thought to give the user personal protection. Shields were often passed down through the generations. Decorated buckskin covers protected them.

Storytelling

Many Crow stories center on Old Man Coyote. This character is often portrayed as a trickster. Old Man Coyote is also considered the creator of the world and of the Crow people.

CUSTOMS

Male bonding

When they became adults, most Crow men joined a sodality, or voluntary men's organization. The members of these groups had a special, family-like bond with each other. There were often intense rivalries between different sodalities. The two most popular were the Lumpwoods and the Foxes.

Festivals and ceremonies

The Sun Dance was the most sacred traditional Crow ceremony. Sun Dances were held to help a man to receive a special vision, usually so he could cure a sick child or get revenge on an enemy. The man who held the Sun Dance was called the whistler. He asked for the help of a shaman who had a sacred doll. The dolls were seen as gifts from the gods. They were passed down from one generation to the next.

Other men who sought visions could take part in the Sun Dance. To do so, they fasted and inflicted wounds on themselves. For many years, the U.S.

Most Crow men developed strong ties with other members of their group of sodality.

Each August, Crow Agency becomes the "Tepee Capital of the World" when the Crow hold a giant celebration there.

government did not allow traditional Crow ceremonies. The Sun Dance was brought back in 1941 by William Big Day. Today, it continues. The Crow hold two or three Sun Dances each summer, with up to 100 participants.

Every year, during the third week in August, Crow Agency becomes the "Tepee Capital of the World." The Crow hold a giant homecoming. It features powwows (celebrations of native songs and dances), arts and crafts shows, a rodeo, and a road race. This celebration has been held for more than 90 years. Food booths sell frybread, Indian tacos, and traditional menudo, a mixture of chili and tripe (part of an ox's stomach). Other popular treats are puffball mushrooms and blueberry pudding.

Vision quest

Traditionally, a young man went
on a vision quest to connect with
his guardian spirit. First, he
purified himself in a sweat lodge.
Then, he traveled to a sacred site
on a mountaintop. There, he
consumed no food or water for
three days and slept uncovered in the cold for three
nights. Some vision seekers cut off the first joint of
one finger and offered it to the rising sun. On the
fourth day, after the young man had proved his
courage, his guardian spirit would come to him in
a vision. It would give the man a sacred song or a
symbol that he could use to ask for help in the future.

Crow men went
on vision quests
to contact their
guardian spirits.

Courtship and marriage

In Crow culture, girls usually married at a young age.
Young men could not hunt until after they were
married. As a result, they spent most of their time
grooming themselves to show off for eligible young
women. To propose marriage, a man offered horses
to the girl's brothers and meat to her mother. Some
Crow men had more than one wife.

Current tribal issues

Like many other tribes, the Crow have been
involved in a number of land claims and disputes

over the years. They are concerned about how their lands are used. They feel that non-Indians profit from their land too often.

The plots of land that tribal members received in the early 1900s were not enough to support the growing population. A father might split his land among his children at his death. Later, they divided their portion among their children. After a while, some pieces of land were divided so many times that the individual plots were smaller than an acre. This made it difficult to farm or ranch. As a result, much of the reservation land was sold or leased to large farming or mining companies.

The Crow have found it hard to get what they believe is a fair amount of the income from the use of their natural resources. They did receive a $9.2 million land claim settlement from the U.S. government in 1961. They also got another $2 million in 1963 for their Yellowtail Dam and Reservoir property. The Crow used this money to buy land, to start industrial development programs, and to make loans to tribal members. In recent times, the tribe has made plans to invest in a trout farm, a hog-raising operation, and a power plant.

In 1963, the U.S. government awarded the Crow $2 million for property near the Yellowtail Dam and Reservoir.

Notable people

Plenty Coups (c. 1848–1932), or Alaxchíiaahush ("Bull That Goes Against the Wind"), was the last traditional chief of the Crow. Plenty Coups represented the Crow before the federal government. In 1921, the chief was chosen to represent all Native Americans at the dedication of the Tomb of the Unknown Soldier near Washington, D.C.

Curly, a Crow scout

Other notable Crow include: scout Curly (c. 1859–c. 1935); educator and administrator Barney Old Coyote (1923–); and president of Little Big Horn College Jeanine Pease-Windy Boy (1949–).

For more information

Frey, Rodney. *The World of the Crow Indians: As Driftwood Lodges.* Norman: University of Oklahoma Press, 1987.

Lowie, Robert H. *The Crow Indians.* Lincoln: University of Nebraska Press, 1983.

Wood, Leigh Hope. *The Crow Indians.* New York: Chelsea House Publishers, 1993.

Glossary

Reservation land set aside and given to Native Americans

Ritual something that is custom or done in a certain way

Sacred highly valued and important

Shaman a priest or priestess who uses magic for the purpose of curing the sick, divining the hidden, and controlling events

Tradition a custom or an established pattern of behavior

Treaty agreement

Tribe a group of people who live together in a community

Index